Rachel on the Run

Also by Maggie Prince

In the Leapfrog series:

DRAGON IN THE DRAINPIPE
DRAGON IN THE FAMILY
THE GLORY HOLE

In Brock Books:

WISHING POWDER

Published by Abelard:

WITCH HILL

Rachel on the Run

MAGGIE PRINCE

Hodder & Stoughton
LONDON SYDNEY AUCKLAND TORONTO

British Library Cataloguing in Publication Data

Prince, Maggie
Rachel on the run.
I. Title
823'.914[J] PZ7

ISBN 0-340-33806-7

First published 1984
Second impression 1987

Published by Hodder and Stoughton Children's Books, a division of Hodder and Stoughton Ltd, Mill Road, Dunton Green, Sevenoaks, Kent TN13 2YJ

Photoset by Rowland Phototypesetting Ltd, Bury St Edmunds, Suffolk

Printed in Great Britain by T. J. Press (Padstow) Ltd, Padstow, Cornwall

Chapter 1

The impact as the oncoming lorry hit them was louder than anything Rachel had ever heard before. With a crunch the side door concertinaed. The bonnet crumpled like screwed-up paper. Rachel saw it happening in the split second that she hurtled through the shattered windscreen. She felt almost detached as though it were happening in slow motion. Then her head hit the tarmac and everything went black.

When she forced her eyes open again she knew that only moments had passed. The roadway, everything, whirled sickeningly. She wondered dazedly what she was doing here. Through a mist she saw the lorry, buckled at one side, pulling into the opposite verge. On her side of the road a black car lay on its side, two wheels spinning crazily. Rachel dragged herself to her feet and looked around furtively. She did not know what she was doing here, but one thing she did know. She must escape while she had the chance. She began to stagger away from the scene of the accident. A side road beckoned, and a verge with soft green grass. Rachel felt herself falling.

Rachel woke up in a ditch. Her head ached and her arms felt stiff and numb. Tall grass waved around her head and sunlight seeped down on to her face through the branches of a hawthorn tree which grew over the ditch. She knew it was a hawthorn. She recognised the leaves. But, appallingly, she did not recognise herself. With a jolt of horror the girl in the ditch realised that she did not know who she was.

She sat up with difficulty, trembling. The ditch was dry and the air was warm. It must be summer.

Who am I? Why am I here? She stared down at herself. She was wearing a blue and white striped dress and her arms and legs were covered with scratches. The grazes and cuts were new, with the blood barely dry. Out of the corner of her eye she could see a long strand of wavy brown hair next to her face. It could have belonged to anybody, for all its familiarity. Nearby, the occasional buzz of a car passed by. Their infrequency told her she must be in the country. Yet if she had the sense to know that she was in the country and that the sounds were traffic, how could she not know who she was? And why was she in the ditch?

Slowly she stood up. Her head reeled painfully and she put her hand up to it. Something was sticky. Her head was bleeding. The fingers which had touched her forehead were covered in blood. She must have had an accident. But why wasn't she in hospital?

The ditch was deep and it was an effort to climb out. A wide grass verge separated it from the country road. Behind her was a high hedge and on the opposite side of the road a low drystone wall stretched away towards the hills. Bracken grew against the wall and nearby the sound of a stream could be heard. Rachel knew somehow that she was in the north.

A glint of metal around her wrist caught her eye. She sat down on a moss-covered stone and examined it. It was a bracelet with silver links and a flat strip. RACHEL was engraved on the flat strip.

So she was Rachel. The name did sound vaguely familiar. She began to feel desperately afraid. Rachel who? She knew so much. She knew the plants. She recognised herb robert growing out of a crevice in the stone. She knew she must be suffering from amnesia. But everything about her personally was just out of reach.

The road where cars were passing sounded nearby, so Rachel stood up and made her way carefully towards it. The side road with tufts of grass growing through its disintegrating surface gave way to a smooth well-kept main road. A6, said a notice on the far side. Suddenly Rachel peered across the road, her heart pounding. On the opposite verge lay a small heap of shattered glass. It was windscreen glass smashed into the characteristic shape of small pebbles. So there *had* been an accident.

Suddenly she heard another car approaching. Without knowing why, she ducked behind the crumbling roadside wall and watched between the stones. A white Range Rover with a dark blue light on top slowed to a halt and two men got out. Rachel stifled a scream. Police. She shut her eyes and buried her face in the musty dried leaves which lay by the wall. She knew it was her they were after, yet she couldn't remember why. She knew that at all costs they must not find her.

There was a clank of metal.

'Don't suppose it'll do much good, Bert,' said one of the men, then a car door slammed and the Range Rover drove away.

After several minutes Rachel emerged from her hiding place. A notice now stood by the roadside. POLICE APPEAL: WOULD ANYONE WHO WITNESSED AN ACCIDENT BETWEEN A BLACK AUSTIN PRINCESS AND AN ARTICULATED LORRY AT THIS SPOT ON TUESDAY THE 1ST OF JUNE AT 6.30 P.M. PLEASE CONTACT THE POLICE AT ROWNSIDE POLICE STATION OR DIAL 999.

Chapter 2

Rachel decided to get away as fast as possible. She listened for a moment to hear from which direction the sound of water was coming. She would look a lot less conspicuous when she had washed the blood off her injuries. It sounded as though the stream were in a dip in the next field on. She ran stumbling towards the far low stone wall and began to climb over it. Its loose mossy stones rocked beneath her feet.

'Blimey!' said a voice. 'What does the other feller look like?' Rachel fell off the wall into the tussocky field on the far side. Furiously she stared up at the brown-skinned boy who was watching her.

'You mind your own business,' she said icily, and got up with as much dignity as she could muster.

The boy, who was about her own age and dressed raggedly, shrugged. 'Sorry. It's just you looked like a spook, coming over the wall white-faced and dripping with blood. Are you all right?'

Rachel glared savagely. 'At least I know only to spook when I'm spoken to.' She turned and ran to where brown peaty water gushed over flat stones lower down the slope. The stream ran parallel with the main road. On the far side of the steep bank sheep grazed among the bracken. When Rachel looked behind her again the boy had gone.

The water was cool. Rachel had taken off her shoes and socks and had one foot in it when she heard the bellow.

'Oy!'

It was a huge, red-faced farmer advancing towards her on the other side of the stream. 'Oy there! Get away, yer damn gipsies! After me trout again are yer?' He waded into the stream in his muddy green wellingtons and Rachel leapt back.

'No, I'm not,' she stammered. 'I-I just wanted to wash my face.' She half turned to run.

'Get back to yer caravans, yer heathen!' The farmer had gone purple in the face. 'Damn gipsies.' He picked up a stone from the stream and threw it at her. Rachel fled. 'Get back to Rownside! I don't want Rownside's problems over here! Little devils!'

Rachel almost fell over the boy as she ran. He was crouching behind a clump of coarse grass. In his hand was a catapult with the rubber band pulled taut. Despite everything Rachel began laughing as she ran.

She was out of breath and still laughing when she reached the bridge. Puffing, she stopped and leaned against the cool damp stones. There was no sign of the farmer behind her, or of the boy.

She scanned the field carefully, then tucked her dress into her knickers and crept under the bridge to where the water flowed fast and dark. It was like an anaesthetic on her scratched arms and legs. She screwed her eyes shut and put her face in too. Her hair streamed out with the current and the wound on her forehead ached with the cold. Traces of blood drifted away. If only she had a comb and a mirror. There, she thought incredulously. I know about combs and mirrors. I can even remember a two-sided brown tortoiseshell comb I had. It seemed very odd that she could remember all this yet not know who she was.

The water glittered darkly below the bridge, and a blurred image of her face came and went on its surface. If she could see herself would she remember everything? She felt her face. Her hands were thin and tanned. Her face was just . . . a face. It didn't feel recognisable or familiar at all.

Feeling cleaner, she emerged into the sunshine. Peewits soared overhead calling. Eeee-it. Eeee-it. There were no other sounds apart from the occasional whirr of a car passing on the road above the bridge. The sun began to dry her skin and hair. She noticed that her dress was torn at one side. Had it happened in the accident? She didn't feel as though she normally wore torn dresses. She felt in her pockets but there was nothing in them. She had no money for food or for anything else. At the thought of food

Rachel's stomach gave an enormous twinge. How long was it since she had eaten? She had no idea. She thought of meat and potatoes, rice pudding, oranges, pancakes, baked beans on toast. She began to feel quite ill with hunger, and realised she would probably have to steal to survive.

Firstly, though, she must get further away from the scene of the accident. When the police came looking for her, which she knew with a fearful certainty that they would, this would be the area they would search. With her head still aching slightly she walked up the slope beside the bridge and climbed over the wall at the top. A signpost pointed to Rownside one way, Kendal another, and the remaining arm said PENDERDALE 2 MILES. Rownside was no good. That was where the police and the little devils were. Kendal was too far. She set off towards Penderdale.

Chapter 3

Penderdale was on the coast. Rachel was amazed to find that the small, grey stone village had a short promenade with green-painted iron railings and a steep drop to the flat muddy sand and the sea. Further along, the sand formed pools and gulleys with tufts of marram grass and sea pinks blowing beside them. The village appeared to be on a bay. In the distance tree-lined cliffs curved round and away. On the promenade a few small tourist shops catered for a few large tourists.

Rachel walked along slowly, her stomach rumbling. She tried to look as though she belonged to someone and had somewhere to go.

On a corner she noticed some public lavatories. Surely there would be mirrors there. Her heart thumping with excitement she crossed the road and went in.

There was one mirror. A tall, broad woman in a crimplene trouser suit blocked it entirely. Rachel hesitated, then unable to wait any longer to see the face which belonged to her, she muttered, 'Excuse me,' and peered round the woman's shoulder. The woman leapt to one side.

'Eeee!' she bellowed. 'You young girls are vain!'

But Rachel was staring transfixed at the face which was hers. It was not familiar.

It was thin and had blue eyes. Its wavy hair was a mess and a huge bruise showed below its fringe. The wound itself was hidden by hair.

'Excuse me,' she said once more to the tall woman, who was teasing her hair up into pinnacles on her head then smoothing them over into a stiff grey helmet. 'Could I possibly borrow your comb?'

Rachel realised at once that this had been a mistake. The woman drew in a whistling outraged breath, then turned and stamped out of the shabby little room.

Rachel sighed and had a drink of water at the tap, then washed the gash on her head again and dried it on a paper towel. Back outside in the sunshine she looked around. On the opposite side of the road, next to the green railings, a man with a cart was shouting, 'Morecambe Bay shrimps! Morecambe Bay shrimps!' Rachel's mouth watered. She crossed to the cart. A man was buying a bag each for his four children.

'Give 'em a bag each,' he said to the stallkeeper. 'How much is that?'

Rachel lined up behind the four children. When the stallkeeper got to her he kept on dishing out the shrimps and handed her a bag too. The last of the four children eyed her curiously.

‘They’re more expensive than last year,’ grumbled the father, handing over the money. Rachel raced away with her shrimps, weaving in and out between the people who strolled along the promenade.

‘Hey!’ she thought she heard a voice shouting behind her, but she wasn’t sure.

Where the promenade ended a narrow lane began, snaking upwards towards the top of the cliffs. Rachel climbed over the crumbling wall which separated it from the band of trees bordering the cliffs, and walked through the green shade eating her stolen shrimps.

The tiny boiled fish were pink and curly, and tasted powerfully of the sea. Rachel gobbled them down. They were not enough. Nearby she saw some wild raspberries growing. She ate those too. It was round about then that she began to feel she was being watched. She looked back over her shoulder. The woods were very still and quiet. No-one was visible.

Feeling tense and afraid, Rachel made her way back to the lane. The corner of her eye caught a flash of white, but when she spun round no-one was there. She told herself she must be imagining things. Further up the lane a small green signpost said FOOTPATH TO ROWNSIDE HEIGHTS. On the stile beneath the signpost someone had dropped half an egg sandwich. Rachel picked it up, dusted it down, and ate it. When she straightened up, a man was watching her. His arm was in a sling. His face was so familiar that Rachel's blood ran cold.

'Hello Rachel,' he said quietly. 'Inspector Smith always finds who he's looking for.'

Rachel gave a scream and ran. She raced up the lane, then swerved off into the woods. The undergrowth was thick here and she had to fight her way through, gasping as briars whipped her across the face. She didn't dare to waste time looking back, but she could hear the man crashing along behind her. Surely she must be near the top of the cliff now. Suddenly the trees thinned and the ground sloped away steeply to the sand. The noise of pursuit became fainter. Rachel skidded down the incline between the brambles, and swung with an arm-stretching jolt on a gnarled hawthorn at the bottom. There was just a short jump to the sand. A weatherbeaten notice board leaned drunkenly nearby, but there was no time to read it. Rachel looked once more behind her, then jumped and ran along hunched down, parallel with the bottom of the cliff.

Chapter 4

Far away on the sands sheep grazed, munching the tufty grass. Nearer where she ran small pools flashed with tiny fish. In the distance where the water shimmered, shrimp fishers were turning their tractors towards home. The sun went behind a cloud and stayed there. The perspiration dried on Rachel's arms and face and she began to feel cold. Where was the dreaded Inspector Smith now? She stopped, fighting for breath, and leaned against the white limestone cliff. No sound came from behind or above her. Cautiously she let her eyes travel from side to side. Would it be any use shouting for help from the shrimp fishers if Inspector Smith were suddenly to appear? Probably not. Why should they help her instead of the police? She stood back and gazed up at the cliff, and suddenly she saw the cave.

She recognised it instantly, and felt weak with shock. It was a yawning gap in the cliff above the level of her head. For a moment she thought she would remember everything. She knew that cave. She knew the way the trees lowered down at her from the top of the cliff. She remembered being in the cave and finding the skull of a sheep. But when? When?

It was no good. It had gone, the familiarity and the tantalising half-memory. It began to rain, a fine, cold drizzle which soaked her clothes in seconds. She started climbing up the slippery rockface towards the cave entrance. Her feet and hands found safe crevices as though they knew the way on their own. Yet how could she possibly know this place when she had come here by accident?

At last she heaved herself into the cave's mouth. A dank, sour smell greeted her. She wrinkled her nose in disgust and sat in the entrance while she got used to it. The rain fell like a curtain now and there was no sign of Inspector Smith. Rachel wondered again what she could possibly have done, for the police to be after her. She could remember vaguely feeling guilty, people being angry with her. But why?

After a while Rachel ventured further inside. The cave was dark and deep further on, narrowing into a sort of waist, then broadening out again into a wider cavern beyond. Here the smell was overwhelming and Rachel gasped for air. Gradually her eyes became used to the dimness. Cigarette ends littered the floor and an empty Coke can lay in a corner. A sock lay there too. How strange, and where was the other one? Maybe a one-legged man had been washing his foot in Coke. At least everything seemed dry. Dusty, sandy deposits lay on the floor and ledges of the cave, so obviously the tide did not wash in here. Even the smell did not seem too bad after a while. This would do nicely as a temporary shelter while she thought what to do next.

She thought again about Inspector Smith. Had his arm been in a sling because he had been in the same accident as her? Had he been taking her away to prison when his black Austin Princess had crashed? Rachel dozed, then slept, shivering in the night, but not waking.

It was the shuffling sounds which woke her. Rachel's eyes snapped open. Dim morning light was filtering in to where she lay huddled by the cave wall. Slowly and fearfully she sat up. It sounded as though a large animal were moving in the outer section of the cave. Her mind returned first to the skull of the sheep, and she wondered if it had come back to haunt her. Then with a quiver of horror she remembered Inspector Smith and his sling. He would shuffle clumsily up a cliff-face, wouldn't he?

A loud snort made her jump. Abruptly the light was blocked out and the whole of her section of the cave was plunged into darkness. Rachel scrambled to her feet.

'Oy, is someone there?' demanded a slurred male voice. She nearly collapsed with relief. It was not a ghost and it was not Inspector Smith.

Light returned to the opening, and after the total darkness it dazzled her. Then a huge flapping figure emerged from the shadows.

'Oy, I said. Who's there? I ain't scared of no bogies. Come out bogey and I'll get yer.'

The man was drunk. The smell of him was

suffocating, even worse than the smell of the cave.

'It's all right,' croaked Rachel. 'I'm not a bogey.' The figure peered at her with difficulty.

'A lass eh? 'Pon me soul. A lass. Gippo are yer?'

'Er, yes.'

'Yeah. Well yer'd hardly be the queen of Sheba shacked up here, would yer?'

'Er, no.'

The figure crashed heavily down into the furthest corner of the cave so that the light fell on him, and Rachel saw that he was a tramp. His stained, grey macintosh was tied with string around his middle, and he had a huge sheet of polythene wrapped across his shoulders. In his hand was a half-empty bottle of strong-smelling liquid.

He fingered the polythene.

'Keeps yer warm, this does. Dry too. Put it round yer. Yer look cold, lass. Here.'

Rachel was cold, but she was also afraid of the man.

'No, it's all right thank you. I must go.'

'Blimey, you've got fancy manners. "I must go",' he mimicked.

As he spoke a sound came from outside. It was the rattle of small stones dislodged and bouncing down the cliff.

Chapter 5

Despite the state he was in, the tramp heard it too. He cocked his head suspiciously. Shoe soles squeaked on wet stone. Rachel flattened herself against the rockface at the back of the cave.

'Flippin' nosey-parkers,' muttered the tramp.

'It's probably the police,' Rachel mouthed frantically. The tramp's eyes widened. He heaved himself heavily to his feet and lumbered towards the entrance.

'Oy!' he shouted. 'Gerroff! Gerrout of it!'

'Oh, good morning.' The smooth tones were those of Inspector Smith. From where she cowered, Rachel could see the silhouette of the tramp in the cave entrance. He began scratching vigorously.

'Flippin' fleas. Flippin' bugs.' He hawked and spat. 'Yeah? What d'yer want?'

A few more stones tumbled down the cliff. 'Oh, er, I wondered if you'd seen my little girl anywhere around here. She's dark-haired, about twelve, and wearing a blue and white dress.'

'Ain't seen nobody at all. I eat little girls for breakfast. She'd better see me before I see her.' He gave a wheezy titter and turned back into the cave. Slowly, with slithers and clatters, the noise of the intruder retreated.

Rachel held her breath. The tramp started to snort convulsively, and held on to his chest. 'Flippin' police. His little girl. Codswallop!' He keeled over in the corner and went to sleep.

After waiting about half an hour Rachel looked out through the cave mouth. She wondered what time it was. She had no watch. Perhaps it had been lost in the accident, because a pale band circled her wrist, and she kept glancing there as though she normally had one. The wooded bay stretched round in a gentle curve, empty and still. Cautiously she climbed down the damp rock to the flat, smooth sand. Just before she put her foot down she saw the deep imprints left by the ridged soles of Inspector Smith's shoes. If he had left footprints, then so would she. She edged herself carefully on to a clump of grass, then jumped from there into one of the shallow pools. She would be safer away from the shore line, cutting across the bay. She made her way via the grass and pools in a diagonal line away from the cliffs. She didn't notice at first that the ground was becoming softer, although when she did leave the pools behind and risked leaving tracks on the wet sand, her sandals squelched loudly and water seeped into the footprints she had left behind. In the distance the notice she had omitted to read the day before was indistinguishable at this range.

Then suddenly it was like going down in a lift. The sand no longer supported her feet. Rachel flung up her arms as she fell forward. The ground had simply opened beneath her. It was quicksand.

As fast as it had opened, the ground lapped back around her. It wrapped itself around her waist and held her legs heavily down as though they were cemented in place. Beneath her feet though the sand continued to give gently. Rachel was sinking.

With a panic-stricken scream she spread her arms flat and tried to flatten the upper part of her body too. This was what you had to do in quicksand, wasn't it? A voice in her head said, 'Great Uncle Joe Walker went down in t'quick-sand, him and his pony and trap and all. They set out to cross the bay and were never seen again.'

Who had said that to her? It was an older voice. A voice like the ones around here, not like hers. 'If you're ever in quicksand don't wriggle and flap. Lie flat and try to edge your way out.' How ironical. She was remembering things now that it was too late. She tried to quell her panic. This couldn't be it, the end of everything.

'Help!' she shrieked. 'Help! Help! I'm sinking!'

In the distance the tide turned, a low rippling flood, and came streaming back across the level sands of the bay.

Rachel was shivering violently now. She had sunk up to her armpits, and when she tried to scream her lungs would not expand to take in the air. Suddenly, before her eyes, a thin film of water poured gently across the surface of the sand. Heaven help her, the tide was coming in.

At first she did not hear the rumbling, so great was her terror. When finally she did, it was almost upon her. Ten metres away a tractor trundled by, leaving deep welts behind it.

Rachel howled. Somehow, despite the restricting sand, she made her voice louder than the roar of the tractor, and the increasing rumble of the two others which she realised were following it.

'Help! Help! I'm sinking!'

For a moment she thought they had not heard her as the tractors continued on their way, then abruptly one engine cut out.

'Bloomin' 'eck!' A man jumped down and came a few steps towards her, then hesitated. 'Hey Donald! Over here! There's a lass trapped in t'quicksand.'

Donald came running from one of the other tractors, which had now stopped, and brought a thick rope with him. Rapidly his huge calloused hands tied it into a large lasso, then he deftly threw it so that it whistled through the air and landed over Rachel's head.

'Get yer arms through that, lass. Don't fret. We'll have you out.'

Frenziedly Rachel struggled to get the noose under her arms. Her movements sucked her deeper into the quicksand. Then the rope pulled tight.

'Tie it on t'tractor, Tom,' said Donald. 'You guide rope and I'll drive t'tractor. Mek it quick.

Tide's coming in fast now. It's all right lass. Hold tight.'

The tractor started to move and the jerk of the rope burned Rachel's armpits.

'Keep yer arms spread out, lass. It's no good if rope comes off.'

Rachel tried to do as he said, but the noose tightening around her chest made breathing almost impossible and she began to feel dizzy and weak. The sky was becoming darker now, and gusts of wind buffeted the waves which were pouring in fast, one after the other. The salty water slopped against her chin and tried to get into her mouth. Slowly the tractor revved forward, and slowly Rachel felt herself moving. An icy wind whipped round her legs. She was out. She was free. With a gobbling sound the sand closed behind her and she was dragged wet and muddy across its surface to where Tom stood waiting to help her up.

'Ee lass, what a to-do. It's a blessing we came by. Come on, I'll help you up on to t'tractor and tek you home.'

Chapter 6

Tom's house was an old, grey stone cottage on the edge of Penderdale, where the woods overlooked the sea. Tom's wife, Mildred, was appalled when she saw Rachel, whose teeth were chattering and who was speechless with cold and fright. Tom explained the circumstances in which they had found her.

'She can't be from hereabouts, then,' said Mildred. 'All the local children know not to go in the quicksands. Funny though Tom, do you notice she has the look of that little Emily up at Walker's Tower Grange?'

'Nay, her hair's darker. I reckon she's from t'gipsy camp over at Rownside.'

'Likely you're right. One thing's sure though. She'll catch pneumonia unless she's put into a hot bath straight away.' Mildred took her firmly by the arm. 'Come along, dear. We'll find out who you are and take you home later. You're blue with cold. Can you tell me what your name is?' She led her towards the bathroom. Suddenly Rachel knew.

'Rachel Cavendish.'

'Oh. Fancy. Well I'll just call you Rachel. Now let's get the water running. While you're in the bath I'm going to find you some warm clothes to put on. I've got all the stuff for the Mothers' Union jumble sale in the garage. There should be something there to fit you. There'll not be a lot left for the sale soon, what with those long johns I gave to the old beggarman yesterday. Never mind. He needed them poor old chap, all wrapped up in his plastic bag. And you need some nice warm trousers too, wandering about in a thin torn dress in this weather.' Mildred went off tut-tutting and Rachel got into the bath.

The water was almost unbearably hot and at first Rachel thought she would pass out, but later when she was sitting by the fire wrapped in Mildred's dressing gown and drinking hot tea and whisky, she began to feel very good indeed.

'We shouldn't be needing fires at this time of year, should we Rachel?' said Mildred, sitting down opposite her. 'I don't know what the weather's coming to. Here, I've made us all some toasted cheese sandwiches. Can you manage some?' Rachel had trouble getting out a polite thank you before she fell on them ravenously. Tom came and joined them. He had discarded his gumboots and put on a pair of tartan slippers, but still smelt very fishy.

'Are you from t'gipsy camp, Rachel?' he asked.

Rachel was sorry to have to lie to them after they had been so kind, but if they knew she had lost her memory they would certainly call the police. For a moment, bone-chilling terror returned to her.

'Er, yes,' she replied.

'You don't sound like a gipsy to me, dear.' Mildred eyed her piercingly.

'Oh well, er . . .'

She was saved by the arrival of Donald, who had come to find out how she was and to offer her a lift back to the gipsy camp at Rownside.

'I expect your Mam'll be worried sick wondering where you are,' he said.

Rachel wondered. Was there perhaps a mother worried sick about where she was? How could she possibly not remember her own mother?

She thanked Tom and Mildred for all they had done. They watched her anxiously and seemed reluctant to see her go. From the bottom of the path Rachel looked back at the warmth and safety of the cottage and blinked back tears. She was now wearing a pair of jeans and a jumper from the Mothers' Union jumble, and she carried her mud-stained dress in a plastic bag under her arm. On her feet was an old pair of wellingtons. Her sandals had been lost in the quicksand.

It was late afternoon as Donald's car twisted and turned along the narrow lanes. Ten minutes after leaving Penderdale they emerged on to high open ground. In the distance Rachel could see a cluster of caravans.

'Here we are,' said Donald. 'D'you want me to come and put things right with your Mam?'

Rachel shook her head. 'No thanks. She has ten other children to worry about so I don't suppose she's missed me. Thank you very much for the lift, and for rescuing me.'

'Think nowt of it, lass. Tek care.' With a wave and a blast on his horn he was gone. Watching his car disappear into the distance Rachel felt more alone than she had ever done in her life.

For a few moments she toyed with the idea of actually going to the gipsy camp, but the thought of so many strange faces was too frightening. No, she had better make her way back to the safety of the cave on the shore. Perhaps the old tramp would have gone by now, in his flapping polythene and Mothers' Union long johns. Anyway even if he was still there he had been harmless, and he had protected her from Inspector Smith. She wondered briefly why someone as important as an inspector was after her. Could she, Rachel, possibly be quite a dangerous criminal? She struggled desperately to remember as she stood with the moorland wind blowing through her hair. It was no good. Her mind was a blank.

The cloudy weather would make it dark early today and it was a long way back to the coast. Rachel looked towards the circle of caravans. A warm, rich smell of cooking drifted to her nostrils. She turned and walked in the opposite direction.

Chapter 7

Rachel spent the night in a barn. She climbed between the bales of hay to a space at the back, where an old scythe hung on the wall and a heap of ancient sacks lay on the floor. Moonlight gleamed through the arched stone entrance and glinted on the yellow bales. A small gap in the sagging roof showed the stars far above her. The wooden rafters creaked and the bales rustled and quivered. Rachel wondered whether there were rats among the hay. Shivering, she crept under the sacks and fell into an uneasy sleep.

In the small hours she began to dream. She was at school. She was coming out of school in her blue and white uniform. Her bag was heavy and she felt rather cross. Miss Pringle had told her off for wearing a bracelet to school, and she had done rather badly in her maths test.

'Goodbye Samantha,' she called to her friend at the corner of the long lane which led to home. There was a car in the distance. It was coming towards her. It was stopping. A face looked out. It was Inspector Smith. Rachel woke screaming.

It was morning and sunlight streamed in through the barn door. Nearby, chickens clucked. Rachel sat up and looked round. Her legs itched so she pulled up her trouser legs to scratch them. Several fleas leapt high into the air and disappeared. Rachel gasped in disgust and jumped to her feet. Her arms itched too. She looked at them closely and found that they were covered with tiny red bites. That was all she needed, fleas. She shook herself hard and flapped at her clothes. No more fleas appeared, so eventually she sat back down on the sacks to think about her dream.

It had been so vivid, almost as though it had really happened. Was she remembering? Was remembering going to be painful?

'Hey up! Hey up!' Rachel nearly collapsed as a gruff voice shouted suddenly, close by. It was joined by the sound of many shuffling, trudging feet. A large shadow darkened the doorway. Rachel edged herself back behind the bales, but it was only a cow. It was followed by another and another until the whole herd had ambled past the barn door. Rachel crouched down, praying that the farmer would not come in. How could she explain having spent all night in his barn? Her back and legs ached from sleeping on the hard floor and it was with relief that she finally stood up again and stretched.

Gently, from behind, a hand came round and clamped itself over her mouth. Rachel's brief muffled scream was barely out before another strong arm like a whiplash seized her round the waist.

'Quiet!' hissed a ferocious voice.

The muscles which held her felt like iron, yet the figure behind her seemed strangely small. For a moment Rachel went limp, then as the arms which held her also relaxed their grip she brought both her elbows back hard into the ribs of her attacker. As his breath went out with a whistling gasp, Rachel swung her body sideways so that they both lost their balance. They hit the floor together and rolled among the loose straw. Rachel spun round and shot to her feet, expecting to see Inspector Smith. Instead, groaning on the ground, lay the boy she had seen two days before. Rachel tensed her foot, ready to kick him if he should try to attack her again. His jeans were old and torn and his hair matted and dirty. An unwelcome twinge of sympathy stirred in Rachel. At last the boy stopped rubbing his bruised chest and looked up at her accusingly.

'You could have broken my ribs.'

Rachel stared indignantly. 'You started it! I nearly died of fright when you grabbed me.'

'I didn't want you to scream when you saw me and get the farmer over here.'

Rachel gave him a look of polite incredulity. 'You could have said "don't scream".'

'Aye well, what are you doing here any road?'

'Mind your own business. What are *you* doing here?'

'I been out rabbiting. Have you run away from the orphanage?'

'No. I must go. Goodbye.'

'Hang on, what's your name? Mine's Leon.'

'Leigh-on-Sea?' enquired Rachel sarcastically over her shoulder as she left.

'Just a minute. Don't go. There's been someone looking for you, asking about you. He was up at the caravans last night.'

Thank goodness she hadn't gone there. Rachel paused.

'Did you say anything to him?'

'I didn't, but me old Gran who's off her trolley told him she'd seen someone just like you in Kendal. She ain't been to Kendal for ten years, but he believed her.'

'Good old Gran.'

'He said he was the fuzz. What have you done? I won't tell.'

'Pushed a nosy boy over a cliff.'

'Oh, suit yourself then. Are you sleeping in this barn regular? If I see this bloke again I can set him off on the wrong track.'

Rachel wondered if she could trust him. She scratched her flea bites and hesitated.

'Listen, er, Leon. If I tell you and then I find out that you've told anyone else I'll kill you, do you understand? If you knew what the police were after me for you'd know I mean it. I'm hiding in a cave over near Penderdale.'

'Blimey that's a bit obvious ain't it, er, whatsyername?'

'Rachel.'

'Rachel. Everyone knows about them caves.'

'Oh well, that's just too bad. I have a friend

there who knows how to protect me.'

'Have you now. I can show you a quick way back there if you like.'

'No thanks. I have to go and find some food. I'm famished.'

'D'you want me to bring you a flask of tea then?'

Rachel paused and looked back through the barn door. *Could* she trust him?

'Actually Leon, that would be very nice. I'd like a cup of tea more than almost anything.'

As she ran away across the fields she thought to herself, honestly, fancy risking capture for the sake of a cup of tea.

Chapter 8

Rachel followed a narrow crumbling-edged road across the moors until she came to a signpost which said ROWNSIDE 2 MILES, PENDERDALE 4 MILES. She was desperate with hunger. There was no way she could walk four miles. She began to run towards the village which held the police station and the little devils.

The first houses she reached looked large and expensive. They were set at the top of steep, terraced gardens. A baker's van emitting a heart-stopping smell of fresh bread was parked outside one of them. The back of the van was open and the baker was at the top of one of the gardens. Before Rachel even realised she was going to do it she had snatched a loaf and a cream cake from one of the trays, and run. She felt sick with fright as she raced into the shelter of a clump of trees further down the road on the opposite side, but no-one was after her. There were no shouts or pounding footsteps. Nothing. It was eerie. Gradually her pulse slowed and she began to eat what she had stolen. What had been the name on the van? Bardwell the Baker. She sighed. She was clearly becoming more of a criminal all the time. But what could she do? She needed the food more than Mr Bardwell did.

Rownside was larger than Penderdale and not on the coast. In the centre of the village, by the market cross, a signpost said PENDERDALE 2 MILES. At least she would be able to find her way back to the cave.

The shops were beginning to open for the day as Rachel walked through Rownside. A scrawled notice on a door attracted her attention. The shop was a newsagent's and the notice said WANTED – BOY OR GIRL FOR PAPER ROUND. Rachel hesitated. Here was a way for her to earn money for food, instead of stealing. She smoothed down her clothes and went in.

The counter was strewn with magazines and newspapers. Bottles of sweets lined the shelves at the back. With the opening of the door a bell rang far away in the rear of the shop. At once heavy footsteps began to approach. Rachel waited apprehensively. A massive figure loomed in the intervening doorway. Rachel's heart sank disbelievingly. Oh no, it was the woman in the crimplene trouser suit.

She stared at Rachel expressionlessly. Rachel's heart thudded. Had she been recognised?

'Yes?' enquired the woman.

'Er, I wanted to apply for the papergirl's job.'

The woman turned her blank face towards the rear of the shop.

'Mr Fish, it's a girl about the paper round,' she called in doom-laden tones. 'Haven't I seen you before?' she demanded suddenly, leaning forward and thrusting her face close to Rachel's.

'Oh, perhaps you've seen me in church,' Rachel replied piously. The woman narrowed her eyes, but at that moment Mr Fish appeared. He was a stooped, white-haired man with wispy eyebrows which hung over his eyes.

'Hello little girl,' he croaked. 'Take her details Mrs Pilsbury. Name? Address?'

Rachel flushed. 'Rachel Cavendish. Er, 4 Rownside Terrace, Penderdale.'

'Eh? Never heard of it. Never mind. Got that Mrs Pilsbury? Age?'

Age, age, thought Rachel frantically. How absurd not to know one's age. Inspector Smith had said about twelve when he spoke to the tramp, so that would have to do.

'Twelve.' She felt herself going red.

Mr Fish leaned across the counter.

'You ain't from the gipsy camp are you? You're very dark-haired.'

'No,' said Rachel firmly. 'My father is descended from the Spanish royal family.' She paused, realising she had possibly gone a little too far, judging by Mr Fish's astonished expression, then she added recklessly and to make up for the piece of invention, 'Not that it should make any difference to you if I were from the gipsy camp.'

The two gaped at her for a moment then the old man laughed.

'We pay fifty pence a morning and a pound on Sundays. We'll take you since no-one else has applied. Be here tomorrow at seven sharp.'

'Thank you.' Rachel was astounded and grateful. It had been so easy. 'Excuse me sir, but this week could I possibly be paid in advance?'

'What?' shouted the woman. Rachel leapt back but the old man was still laughing.

'Cheeky young madam,' muttered Mrs Pilsbury.

'Go on with you Mrs Pilsbury. Get her the money out of the till. That's two pounds for the rest of this week then, Rachel. You'd better be here, mind, or I'll be round to see your Mam and Dad. Go on! Off with you!'

Rachel took the two pounds gratefully and fled.

Chapter 9

By that afternoon Rachel began to feel very dirty. She washed her face and hands at the public washrooms in the square, but it was a warm dusty day and her flea bites itched. Her teeth felt disgusting too, furry and blunt. She spent a little of her precious two pounds on a toothbrush and toothpaste, and used them after she had had a hamburger and Coke for lunch. By then one pound fifty was spent.

The clock in the square said two o'clock when Rachel decided to make her way back to her cave. Two miles was a long way and she felt tired already. She set off down the road signposted PENDERDALE.

Traffic passed her, swishing along rhythmically. There was no pavement and the road was hard and gritty. Rachel's feet began to ache unbearably and she extended her thumb tentatively to see if anyone would give her a lift.

'Never accept lifts from strangers,' said a voice in her head. Rachel stood still in surprise. This was what people's parents said to them, wasn't it? Never accept lifts from strangers. She thought about her dream. Seeing Inspector Smith in it had woken her. She had woken terrified, but behind the terror had been the thought, never accept lifts from strangers, too.

With the memory of Inspector Smith Rachel began looking behind her nervously, and as a result she nearly walked into an open-backed truck parked on a bend. It was full of hedge cuttings and the driver, a dark-haired man with a scarred cheek and a moustache, was just climbing into his cab at the front. The engine revved. Quickly Rachel grabbed the tailboard and swung herself over it, landing on the prickly branches as the vehicle began to move.

'Hey!' a voice behind her shouted. Rachel's heart gave a panic-stricken jolt and she looked back down the road. The old tramp from the cave was running with an uneven, staggering gait towards the moving truck. He would never catch it. It was like seeing someone running for a bus.

'Come on!' urged Rachel, holding out her hand. The tramp put on a superhuman spurt and caught her hand. Rachel dragged. It was like trying to lift a mattress. One of the tramp's legs pedalled the ground and the other waved in the air as he pivoted on the tailboard of the truck. She sat on his shoulder, pressing down hard. He gave a whistling wheeze and fell in.

It took him several moments to recover, but when he did he beamed, showing a total of two teeth at the top and one at the bottom.

'Thanks lass. Nowt like a lift at this time of day. Let's just hope this truck ain't going to Timbuctoo.'

Rachel started to nod in agreement, but just then her attention was diverted. Something had moved among the brambles at her side. It wasn't just the increased acceleration of the truck causing a disturbance. She edged a branch loose and bent it back to hook on the others. As she did so a whiplash struck out at her wrist.

Rachel jerked back with a scream. The tramp made a gargling noise behind her. It was a snake.

Before Rachel could move away the snake struck again. Its fangs hit a rivet in the thick material of her jeans. She rolled away gasping, tearing her skin on the prickles. The truck thundered on. Had the fangs penetrated the material? She felt so scratched by thorns that she couldn't tell whether or not she had a snake bite too. The reptile had withdrawn again into its dark brambly cave among the briars. It was invisible in the patterns of light and shade beneath the quivering leaves. The lorry screeched round a corner and Rachel held on to the side. The tramp huddled in a corner, his mouth opening and shutting like a fish's. Could it be a grass snake? No, she was fooling herself. The black zig-zag on its reddish-brown back had been all too clear. It was an adder, the only poisonous snake native to the British Isles.

The truck roared up a hill. It was going too quickly for them to jump off. Was this road endless? Were there no junctions or traffic lights to make it slow down?

'Keep still,' she whispered to the old tramp. It's our only hope.'

Suddenly the snake struck again, but missed. Its head retreated, undulating to and fro.

'You need to hit the blighter,' the tramp gabbled frantically under his breath. He twisted round awkwardly and poked a spiky stick at Rachel. Rachel edged back and took the stick from him. Just then the lorry sailed over the top of a hill and they could see the sea in the distance. A sharp bend appeared abruptly ahead. Too late Rachel tried to stop herself from sliding sideways and right on top of the snake. It was no good. All the hedge cuttings and the tramp slid in a tumbling rush, and Rachel landed with a crunch at the far side of the truck. The adder's head arched above her as though it were laughing. Frantically Rachel lunged at it with the stick which she was still holding. She missed and the snake coiled itself back to strike again. Rachel stood up in the bucketing vehicle and aimed carefully, then struck with the stick as the adder's head lashed forward. With a thud and a swish the reptile sailed through the air, out of the truck and away over the hedge. Rachel's knees sagged in disbelief. The truck slowed as it approached another bend.

'Come on,' she said to the tramp, pulling him towards the tailboard. 'It may have half a dozen friends in there.'

'Eh? I ain't getting off while it's going.'

'Well I am. Look, that sign says Penderdale.'

She levered herself over the edge and fell into the road, grazing her arms and legs. Painfully she crawled on to the grass verge and sat among the buttercups and daisies, leaning against the Penderdale sign and listening to the retreating roar of the truck. Then she began to detach the trailing brambles and briars which still clung to her clothes. Surely, she thought, there must have been an easier way of getting to Penderdale than this.

Chapter 10

It was strangely familiar, the stony road down to the shore, although on the previous day she had approached the Penderdale coastline from the opposite end. Yet somehow she knew already the steep white outcrops of limestone jutting above the muddy sand, and the precipice of red sandstone on the far side of the road. At the top of the sandstone cliff was a fence. A flat grassy plateau stretched away beyond it and high above it a skylark sang as it soared into the sky. The scenes were like pictures from a book read long ago.

'Great-Granny Walker Peel was the eldest of twenty-one children,' said a northern voice in her head. 'She played in that cave. She was born in yon tower up on the cliff. It's in ruins now, of course. You can see it from the shore, or you can get to it through the Grange gardens.'

Rachel slowed her pace, willing the voice to continue, but it had gone. A tower, the voice had said. Yes, she knew it. There was a tower somewhere here. Perhaps if she could find it she would remember who she was. The tower, she knew, was somehow involved in her past.

She stood motionless, leaning on the dilapidated five-bar gate which led to the shore itself. The road trailed away beyond it into a dusty path of sand and stones. A few drops of rain fell on to her head. Beyond the gate a car was parked where the sand began. As the rain fell more steadily, its engine started and it lurched unevenly over the stones. Rachel opened the gate for it, struggling as the heavy wooden bars sagged on their hinges and scraped the ground. The man who was driving smiled and waved, and the two children in the back watched her. Suddenly one of them peered more closely at her and rolled down the window.

'Hello, Rachel!' he called loudly, waving. Then the car accelerated and was gone.

Rachel watched with shock as the last of its exhaust fumes dispersed in the damp air. The boy had recognised her. She turned and ran away along the deserted beach.

This time she must watch out for quicksand. She would only go where the sheep were, and look out for the danger notices.

She was wet by the time she reached the cave, and she climbed up with her clothes once more sticking soddenly to her back. The smell was as bad as ever, but Rachel felt as though she were coming home. She set out her toothbrush and toothpaste on a dusty ledge, then checked the remaining fifty pence in her pocket. She was hungry, but felt too tired to go up into the village and buy herself anything to eat, so instead she trailed into the darkest section at the back of the cave and sat down. Then she saw the flask and the paper bag. She stared, then leaned over and pulled it towards her. Had some picnicker left it behind? Might there be something to drink remaining in the flask? She was very thirsty. She unscrewed the top. It was full of hot fragrant tea. Leon! Rachel could have cried. She wished she had been politer to him. She scrabbled at the paper package, pulling it open. Nestling amid a welter of clingfilm were two unevenly cut cheese sandwiches. Rachel took her feast to the cave entrance and sat with her feet hanging out into the rain, while the hot tea warmed her insides. The cheese sandwiches were gritty and rather stale, but tasted better than anything she had ever eaten. Feeling full and warm, she curled up by the cave mouth and fell asleep watching the rain go past.

Rachel dreamed. She was standing in the middle of a ruined tower. Someone was with her, but she could not see who.

'Fancy bringing up twenty-one children on the edge of a cliff,' said the person, a girl. 'I expect if anyone was naughty it was whoops, over the edge!'

Rachel laughed in her dream, but something was wrong. The person was behind her. She tried to turn, but rough arms grabbed her and the voice had changed.

'Your mother has been taken to hospital, Rachel dear.' It was Inspector Smith. Rachel moaned and tried to wake up. 'I'm here to take you to her. You must come straight away, dear. I'm afraid it's serious. It's all right. I'm a policeman. Here's my identity card.' One of the arms stretched round her and she saw that it was dressed in Mrs Pilsbury's crimplene trouser suit and was holding a newspaper. Rachel began to struggle.

'Hey lass, steady on. You'll be over the edge in a minute.'

She woke to find herself being pushed. It was the tramp. He was rolling her away from the cave mouth, and Rachel realised that she had slept all night poised precariously above the steep drop to the sand. It was morning, and the tramp stank worse than ever. His eyes seemed glazed and his breath smelt like paint stripper. Rachel wriggled free and the tramp's momentum carried him forward face first into the gravel. He struggled up and propped himself against the cave wall. Rachel saw that his polythene cloak had a huge tear in it.

'Are you all right?' she asked, feeling concerned for him. 'How far did the truck take you?'

He seemed to have trouble in speaking, and reached into his pocket for his bottle. After a deep swig he brightened up.

'Are yer hungry, lass?' he asked, ignoring the previous question. 'I got food in here.' He patted his bulging pocket invitingly. Rachel's stomach contracted. Yes, she was hungry again. The cheese sandwiches seemed a long time ago now.

'I know what it's like to be hungry,' the tramp confided. 'I been so hungry I've eaten grass and sparrers. I've had liver fluke from eating grass and been in hospital with it. Best four weeks I ever had, them were. I've eaten spotty toadstools I've been that hungry. Ee, but those don't half make yer wild. I half killed a man that day.'

'Fly agaric, I expect,' said Rachel, astonished at herself because the words came from knowledge she hadn't known she had. 'Were they red and white?'

'Aye, they were. Blimey, you're a strange one. Fly what you say?'

'Fly agaric. The Vikings used to eat them before they went into battle, to make them wild.'

'That so? Blimey. Vikings. Yer don't say.'

'You know, those toadstools are awfully dangerous. You took a terrible risk in eating them. I know because my mother's a botanist.' A floodgate opened in Rachel's head and she stood up, her eyes wide. 'Yes, yes, she specializes in rare plants. Her name is . . . her name is . . .'

It was gone. The gates snapped shut. Rachel slumped back against the cave wall, drained.

Chapter 11

The old man had stopped listening anyway.

'Ere.' He dragged something out of his pocket. It was a roughly wrapped newspaper parcel. 'Course, yer gotta cook 'em. Can yer make a fire, lass? Me poor old legs is a bit doddery just now.'

Cook 'em? What?

'I haven't got any matches.'

'I got matches. You fetch some wood and a handful of wet mud. Go on with yer.' He took another dribbling mouthful from the bottle. The liquid dripped from his chin.

'All right then.' Rachel turned to go, blinking as the sun shone in at the cave's entrance. The tide was far out and the sands stretched distant and flat, glinting as the rain dried up. The air outside smelled fresh and sweet. Dizzy with a sudden lightening of her spirits Rachel filled her lungs and set off to find driftwood and wet mud.

There were plenty of grey grainy sticks along the base of the cliff and Rachel soon gathered an armful. They felt light and dry. In the distance she could see the shrimp fishers with their tractors. Mud, where could she find mud? What did he want it for? She hadn't thought to ask. There were clayey pockets in the sand and she supposed that this would have to do. She scooped up a handful and turned to go back. At that moment she saw the tower.

It was a whitish, crumbling ruin high on the clifftop above her. Her stomach gave a lurch. It was so familiar. It was the tower from her dream. She knew quite clearly what it looked like inside. There were four ancient stone walls with the unclimbable skeleton of a stairway on one of them. Two ruined hearths stood one at each end, still black with the marks of bygone smoke. Companionship, friendship, and the excitement of exploring were the sensations which went with the memory. Rachel stood and stared, her dream coming back to her. Someone had been with her in the dream, someone she knew well. But they had changed into Inspector Smith who had told her that her mother was ill. Suddenly she knew that he *had* told her her mother was ill. It had happened in real life. Like a jigsaw, it all connected up with her dream of the previous night. The lane, her friend Samantha (of course, *Samantha*), the black car stopping with Inspector Smith in it. 'Rachel Cavendish?' he had asked. "Your mother has been taken to hospital, Rachel dear. I'm here to take you to her.'

Rachel stood staring up at the white tower, willing it to continue helping her to remember, but it was no good. The rest was a blank. She must get up there. Perhaps if she actually stood within the four walls everything would come back to her.

But first she must eat. She felt weak and lightheaded. She shifted her awkward load and turned back towards the cave.

It was a hedgehog. In the old man's newspaper parcel was a dead hedgehog. Rachel recoiled in dismay.

'Yer gotta be quiet and sly to catch these blighters,' grinned the tramp showing his rotten stumps of teeth between cracked lips. ' 'Ere. Give us the mud.'

Rachel slopped it into his dirt-grained hands. He began to paste it daintily on to the hedgehog.

'You light the wood. 'Ere's the matches.'

Rachel caught them squeamishly. She was quite sure she would never be able to eat hedgehog, but on the other hand she might have to get used to this sort of thing if she were to avoid starvation. She heaped the wood together and tried to light it. It refused to burn.

'Use the newspaper, yer great lummox,' shouted the tramp. 'Are yer daft or summat?'

Rachel tightened her lips angrily, but picked up the stained paper with the tips of her fingers. She was about to push it under the wood when her eyes caught one of the headlines. It said KIDNAP CAR FOUND CRASHED. Slowly Rachel spread it out, ignoring the old tramp's grumblings that she should hurry up. She began to read.

"Fears increased today for the safety of the still-unnamed Hertfordshire bank manager's daughter, when the black Austin Princess believed to have been involved in her capture was found abandoned after a crash on the Lancashire-Cumbria border. Police are intensifying their search for those believed responsible . . ." Here the page was torn. Was this it then? Were the police chasing her because she had been involved in the kidnapping of someone?

'Where's the rest of this newspaper?' she demanded of the astonished tramp.

'I dunno, do I?' he growled. 'Found it in t'hedge, didn't I.'

Rachel sighed and flapped her arms impatiently, then scanned the other columns of print. In a column headed NEWS IN BRIEF was the subtitle RANSOM NOTE. Underneath it said "Full story on page six of how the bank manager in the kidnap case was secretly pressurised to steal from his bank to buy his daughter's freedom." Needless to say, page six was not there.

When Rachel looked up again she saw that the old tramp had fallen asleep against the wall with his mouth open. The mud-encrusted hedgehog had rolled out of his hand. She toyed with the idea of searching his pockets for more of the newspaper, but fear of finding something even more revolting stopped her. She stood up, and as she did so a shadow fell across the opening behind her. Rachel jumped up in fright and backed away, turning to face the entrance. It was Leon.

'Hello,' he grinned. 'This your friend, is it?'

'Er, yes. He's a bit tired at the moment.'

'Yeah, tired as a newt from the smell of him. In time for breakfast am I?'

Rachel indicated the prickly corpse.

'Help yourself. Toothpicks provided.'

Leon laughed and began propping the wood expertly into a tent shape over the crumpled newspaper, then he lit it with a match cupped in his hand. The smoke swirled suffocatingly for a moment then drifted out through the cave entrance. Leon collected some wet sand and made a firm ridge of it round the fire, then piled more wood on. It burnt fiercely for a while, the salty smell of the sea in the smoke, then sank down into glowing embers. It was into these that Leon consigned the hedgehog after coating it thickly with more mud. He blew on the embers. Rachel suddenly remembered a barbecue long ago when someone had let her blow on the embers like that.

'Check his pockets. This ain't enough for three,' said Leon. Gingerly Rachel did so and found yet another newspaper-wrapped parcel. Leon went to find more mud while Rachel looked hopefully at the sheet of newspaper, but it was only the sports page.

Later, when the hedgehogs were cooked, the old man woke up and they all ate together sitting in the entrance of the cave by the fire, and watching the tide drain out of the mouth of the bay. The hedgehogs tasted like a cross between rabbit and chicken, with almost fishy overtones, but perhaps, Rachel reflected, as she chewed and chewed repetitively, that was just the salty smell of the distant sea.

Chapter 12

It still felt very early, even when they had finished eating. In some deep recess of her mind Rachel knew that the tide came in about an hour later each day, so from that she worked out that she should leave for her paper round at about the time the tide turned. Leon insisted that she should borrow his bicycle to get to Rownside. He lived at the gipsy encampment, he explained, and at the moment they had some ponies in for selling. He had been riding one of these lately so didn't need his bicycle, although he had come on it this morning.

Rachel was very grateful, and set off for Rownside puzzling the mystery of how she could have been involved in a kidnapping.

She was late.

'This won't do,' grumbled Mrs Pilsbury, her chins wobbling. 'Folks don't like waiting for their newspapers.'

Rachel apologised and set off with the big canvas bag of papers across her back. The job was made difficult by the fact that she did not know the street names, although after she had found the first one the others followed on more easily.

She glanced at the front page of each newspaper as she delivered it, but there was no more about the crashed car or the kidnapping until nearly the last one. What she saw in that made her stop in her tracks. ANGUISH OF BOTANIST, it said. Rachel stood by the gate and began to read. "Barbara Peel, well-known botanist and mother of Rachel Cavendish, said today . . ." At that moment a man rushed out of the house and snatched the newspaper from her.

'You're paid to deliver the newspapers, not read them!' he shouted angrily. 'You've ruined my breakfast!' He stamped off up the path.

Rachel watched him go in desperation. There were no more copies of that particular newspaper in her bag. Her mother, the article had been about her mother. Her mother was anguished, and it must be because she, Rachel, was on the run from the police. She raced round delivering the last two papers then arrived panting back at Mr Fish's shop.

'Do you by any chance have a spare copy of The Times?' she gasped, more than willing to sacrifice some of her precious remaining money for the information it contained. Mr Fish laughed uproariously as though she had made a huge joke.

'All sold out!' he guffawed. 'Have a Beano instead.'

Rachel turned resentfully away and left the shop, but suddenly Mr Fish scurried after her and pressed a bar of chocolate into her hand.

'Don't be late tomorrow!' Mrs Pilsbury called after her.

Rownside was quiet. It was still early and most of the shops were shut. Rachel walked slowly through the centre of the village, wheeling Leon's bicycle and eating the chocolate. It was a relief to get the taste of hedgehog out of her mouth. At the public washrooms she drank a lot of cold water and cleaned her teeth. On her way back round the square she had to pass a squat building with steps up to its blue-painted front door. A notice board stood outside, and above it half embedded in the hedge was a blue sign which said POLICE. Hurriedly Rachel began to walk on by, then for the first time she saw the notice board properly. Her own face looked back at her. Below were the words HAVE YOU SEEN THIS CHILD?

Rachel jumped on the bicycle, her legs like jelly, and began to pedal. She ignored traffic lights and road junctions. She took no notice of vehicles which blew their horns at her, and did not stop until she reached her cave. With sweating fingers she dragged the bicycle up the cliff face after her. The old tramp and Leon had gone and the fire was out. Rachel collapsed sobbing and breathless on to the floor. That was the end of her paper round and the hope of earning more money. Someone could recognise her at any time, now that her photograph was outside the police station.

Rachel's throat and stomach had begun to

ache, and her head was throbbing. Surely she wasn't going to be ill on top of everything else. If only she could remember.

She had nothing more to eat or drink that day, and as night time came she fell into a feverish doze.

Chapter 13

The dreams came straight away. She was at home, a house in the country with the London motorway humming on the other side of the hill. Mum was flat on her stomach in the garden, examining a plant.

'Dad's late home,' she said. 'Have you done your homework, Rachel? You can't go over to Samantha's after tea unless you have.'

Rachel felt unspeakably happy. As she stood there in the warm, sunlit garden Dad's car turned in at the gate.

'Hello darling!' called Mum. 'What has your rotten old bank got that we haven't?'

'Oh, sorry I'm late dear. Several million pounds, since you ask.' He was laughing as he kissed Rachel and she saw him clearly. Slowly, against her will, she woke. The faces of her mother and father were so vivid in her mind that for a moment she felt as though they were with her. Instead only the dark, dirty cave confronted her. Filled with sadness she drifted back into sleep.

She was in another garden. Cultivated lawns and flower beds ran down a slope and gradually merged into woods and brambles. A man was roasting sausages on a barbecue and a woman and a girl sat on the edge of an old well. There was wire netting over the well so that no-one could fall down it, and an ancient bucket no longer used hung over their heads. The door of the large house stood open. Rachel went in.

Inside, the hall was cool and dim. A large portrait hung on the wall opposite the door. In it a man with a black beard stood in the arched window of a white tower. Behind him and far below stretched the waters of the bay, and beyond them the blue Lakeland hills.

'Aye, there's your great great grandfather,' said a male northern voice behind her. 'Raised twenty-one children on the edge of a cliff. There's not many would like to do that these days.'

'No, I should jolly well think not,' replied Rachel in her dream.

'What?' asked a voice close by her ear. 'Jolly well think not what?' Rachel opened her eyes, bewildered for a moment. The sun was shining in through the cave entrance, and Leon was unscrewing a flask. 'Early morning tea,' he grinned. 'Were you dreaming?'

Rachel nodded, finding her throat almost too dry and stiff to move. With difficulty she sat up, the dream still with her.

'Thank you,' she croaked, taking the cup which Leon offered, but scarcely able to drink the hot liquid because of the chattering of her teeth.

'You're ill.' Leon frowned disapprovingly. 'You've caught a cold. Come on. Drink up. It'll do you good.' Rachel drank. 'Listen, you can't stay here like this. You'd better come back with me and my Mam will give you something.'

Rachel stared at him suspiciously. Was he trying to trap her and hand her over to the police? Had he seen her photograph outside the police station? Was there a reward for her capture?

'Go away, Leon. I'm all right. No, I don't mean go away. I'm sorry. And thanks for the tea . . .' She was babbling.

'What's the matter anyway, Rachel? What have you done? It can't be anything they'd send you to prison for . . .'

Rachel interrupted him furiously. 'You don't understand, Leon. I was being *taken* to prison. There's this policeman called Inspector Smith and he was taking me somewhere to lock me up. He told me so. He's the one who came up to your camp. I had to escape from him . . . oh, if only I could remember.'

'Remember? What do you mean?'

'Oh nothing. Forget it.'

'Well if that's all I get for the tea . . .'

'What do you want? A medal? I didn't ask you to bring it.'

You're drinking it though.'

'Oh I'm sorry. Just . . . just don't nag me.'

Leon leaned against the wall.

'OK.' He looked at her thoughtfully. 'You

know, there's something odd about you. Like, you ain't quite with it or something. You ain't got out of a mental home, have you?' Rachel glared at him indignantly and poured herself some more tea, not deigning to answer. 'There's something else odd too. There's a girl who looks ever so much like you, but fairer, lives up in the house near Walker's Tower.'

Walker's Tower! 'Great Granny Walker Peel was the eldest of twenty-one children. She was born in yon tower.' It was the voice from her dream and the words were as clear as if they had just been spoken.

Leon had turned to go.

'I gotta get back. I'll bring you some food later if I can.'

'Leon . . .' Rachel called him hesitantly. 'Leon, I can't do my paper round today. I don't feel well enough. I don't suppose you'd do it for me, would you? I'd give you a share of the money, of course. Don't tell them where I am though.'

'I suppose I could. My Mam won't expect me back till this afternoon. I'd better take the bike then. Which shop?'

Rachel told him, and was surprised at the regret she felt when he left. She finished the tea in the flask and stood up shakily. Her head felt very strange, light and floating. Heat seemed to come and go on her cheeks. She steadied herself. There was one place she must go now. The tower.

Chapter 14

Down on the flat grassy sand Rachel breathed in deeply. She felt dizzy and wobbly. Even if the cliff had not been so steep she would not have been able to climb it in her present state. However, if she went off the shore through the sagging gate and along the top of the cliffs where the woods loomed, perhaps there would be a way through there. On legs which felt like rubber she set off.

There was no visible footpath through the woods, so once she had ducked under the single strand of barbed wire, Rachel pushed her way among the briars and undergrowth. Her sleeves and trousers caught on thorns and branches, and spiders' webs stuck to her face. It was becoming darker. Looking up she saw that the sun had gone in and grey clouds were obscuring the sky. Along the shore it had not seemed far to the tower. Now it seemed miles. Had she missed it? A long stone like that of a gatepost lay in a hollow among dried skeletal leaves. Smaller mounds of whitish rock lay nearby, thistles growing between them. It was lighter. The trees were thinning. Rachel wiped a trembling hand across her forehead. Perspiration dripped into her eyes. Suddenly the woods were a pale glowing green where light shone into a clearing over by the clifftop. She stumbled a few steps more, tripping on the uneven ground, then she came to the tower.

It was small, rectangular, and almost totally ruined. The walls had fallen in until they were barely higher than Rachel's head. At the corners they were almost a metre thick. Around in the undergrowth chunks of them lay where they had crashed among the brambles. At the far side the remains of an arched window looked out across the sea. Rachel stood silently and stared, remembering her dream. Here, once, had stood the man with the black beard while his portrait was painted.

Rachel climbed over the fallen stones and in through the broken doorway. Exhausted, she sat down heavily on a flat boulder and leaned her back against the moss-encrusted wall. Her eyelids drooped and her temperature soared. Heat and shivering chased each other across her shoulders. Her chin sagged forward on to her chest and, like clockwork, the dreams began. It was hot. She was in a hot car, uncomfortable in the back seat. She whimpered in fright. Her hands were tied and Inspector Smith was driving.

'Please let me go, please . . .'

'Shut up.'

The tone was so ferocious that she fell silent. She thought the countryside through which they were passing was familiar. Surely this was the road they travelled when they went on visits to Uncle Roger and Aunt Pauline. If only she could escape here surely they would shelter her. At worst, Cousin Emily could hide her in the ruined tower. Inspector Smith would never find her there. M6, Lancaster, Kendal, the Lakes, the road signs said. Soon it would be too late. Suddenly she noticed the car cigarette lighter in front of her. It was the sort which you pressed in to heat up, then lit your cigarette with when it popped out. Silently she pressed it in with her foot. It seemed to make a very loud click when it popped out after a few seconds, but Inspector Smith did not appear to have noticed.

'I'm going to lie down for a while,' she muttered.

'Thank goodness for that. Maybe I'll have a bit of peace now.'

Rachel lay down and pulled the lighter out with her teeth, then held it hard against the string which bound her hands. The smell was terrible. Surely he must be able to smell it too. As the string singed and parted, he did.

'What's that smell?' he demanded, looking round. It was now or never. Rachel lunged forward and grabbed his left arm, trying to reach the handbrake.

'Why you little . . .'

The car swerved madly, then a lorry appeared, coming towards them round a bend. It hurtled at them and the car buckled like cardboard. Rachel was shocked at the loudness of the thud and the hardness of the impact. She had always thought car crashes involved more of a muffled crumpling, the way it seemed on television. That was all.

Rachel woke with her own scream ringing in her ears. Her mind raced. So that was how the accident had happened. Presumably Inspector Smith had been taken away unconscious or he would have made sure she was recaptured. Too bad he hadn't stayed that way. Suddenly sounds in the woods nearby caught her attention. It sounded like sticks crashing against branches. Faintly, and far off, the sound of men's voices became audible. Nearer, a dog barked.

Rachel had fallen over on to the grass in her sleep. Now she sat up in alarm. Unless she was very much mistaken those were the sounds of a search taking place, and it was coming closer.

Suddenly a dog bayed savagely, almost by her head. Rachel backed away, gooseflesh all over her. Wet snufflings sounded among the leaves. She looked around in panic. At one end of the ruin was a low arched fireplace, with a crumbled heap of stones and a dark crevice at one side. Rachel edged towards it, keeping her eyes on the undergrowth. Her foot dislodged a stone which ricocheted sharply away. At last she was there. The cavity in the thick wall looked dark and suffocatingly small. Would she fit? She lay down and began to wriggle in, feet first. There seemed to be space beneath her feet. Frantically she swung her legs, searching for a foothold. Her toes touched hard stone at one side. Cautiously she pulled the rest of her body in, bruising her ribs on the uneven rock. To her surprise she found that she could stand up. Light filtered in through the hole and she looked around. She was standing on some steps, old worn steps with some sections missing, but a usable stairway nevertheless. This must be the way down to the old cellars.

Suddenly boots crunched next to her ear.

'No sign here, Tom,' said a voice. 'Could have been that young rascal told 'em wrong. He never wanted to go to t'police station in the first place. Mrs Pilsbury had to fair drag him there.'

'Hadn't they seen t'poster?'

'Not till after the lass left yesterday. Course they recognised her straight off then. Mrs Pilsbury was all set to take her to the police station when she came to do t'paper round today, so when the lad came she took him instead. Seems he didn't want to tell, mind you. Could be he's told 'em the wrong place entirely.'

'Aye, could be, but once he knew the whole story, and that there's a reward for her, you'd think he'd be only too keen.'

'If we'd just known the day we pulled her out of t'quicksand . . .'

The voices faded.

It had been her rescuers, Donald and Tom. She could have cried to think that even they would betray her for the sake of a reward. And poor

Leon, whatever had they done to him to make him talk?

Suddenly the dog barked again, close by. Another joined it. Glutinous sniffing noises mingled with the snapping of twigs and rustling of grass.

'Oy! I think they've found the trail again!' an excited voice yelled close by. Horrified, Rachel stared around her in the gloom. She was trapped. The prospect of a fierce dog's massive muzzle appearing in the gap by her head seemed imminent. She looked at the crumbling stairway. Would it support her if she tried to descend it? She took a few cautious steps. It became darker at once. Some of the steps were missing altogether and she had to feel with her feet. Once her foot slipped and small stones went rolling away into the pit, bouncing on and on, fainter and fainter. Surely no-one in their right mind would have had their cellars that far down.

Suddenly she came upon a solid wall of fallen stones. Indistinctly beyond them she could see the outline of a doorway which was completely blocked by what must be the collapsed foundations. That was obviously the entrance to the cellars. There was no way she could get in. But off to her right, where the steps ended in a steep pebbly slope, light seemed to be coming in. She held on to the walls and inched her way towards it down the treacherous gradient. Suddenly the light was bright and there was a sharp bend ahead of her. She allowed herself to skid and skate down the remainder of the slope, landing with her hands against the bend of the rock wall. Just in time she hurled herself backwards, gripping with her hands and feet. Ahead of her lay a sheer drop to the bottom of the cliff.

Chapter 15

It was a narrow crevice caused by erosion and the roots of trees along the clifftop. It would be barely visible from the ground, blending in with the unevenness of the rest of the cliff face. A tuft of delicate blue harebells grew at the opening. Rachel stood on the edge and looked down. The sand and clumps of grass looked far off. The distant sheep looked like toys. She could see the patch of clay where she had collected mud for the tramp the day before. She held on tightly and peered over. There were no footholds in the cliff, and it sloped inwards, away from her. Far behind, echoing eerily, a dog bayed. Rachel gave a shuddering sigh, and jumped.

The cliff flew past in a blur then the ground smashed into her like a giant hammer. Rachel tasted sand in her mouth, or was it her teeth? For a moment whirling star-studded blackness threatened, then she heard a familiar voice saying, 'Rachel? Rachel?'

It was Leon. Rachel opened her eyes and sat up, spitting out sand. He was staring at her in astonishment.

'Blimey Rachel, I thought I'd got used to you, but now you've started dropping out of the sky.'

Rachel began to laugh weakly. Leon looked anxious.

'Are you all right? I had to tell 'em, Rachel. I'm sorry. I had to tell 'em where you were. But it's all different from what you think. You've been on the telly and the radio, and you're in the newspaper.' He waved a copy of the local paper in front of her. She grabbed it. A picture of herself was blazoned across the front page. 'Rachel?' Leon's features seemed to be rippling above her. 'Rachel, the police say they just want to help you . . .'

'Of course they'd say that. That's what Inspector Smith said last time . . .'

'Here, sit up. Are you all right?'

Rachel smiled faintly. 'No,' she said, and passed out.

It was a return journey through the blackness which had blotted out her memory. Once again she came out of school and walked home with her friend Samantha. Her blue and white uniform was creased and it was really too hot to be wearing her blazer, but that was the easiest way of carrying it.

'Goodbye Rachel,' said Samantha as they parted at the top of Rachel's lane.

'Goodbye Samantha.' She watched her friend go. She watched her glance at the black car which slowed, then speeded up again, slowing once more as it approached Rachel. Samantha had a photographic memory for car number plates, and always memorised them just for fun.

'Rachel Cavendish?' Inspector Smith looked out, smiling sympathetically. Rachel nodded, unsmiling and suspicious. Her mother had always emphasized the importance of not speaking to strangers. 'I'm afraid your mother has been taken to hospital, Rachel dear. I'm so sorry. I'm here to take you to her. You must come straight away dear. I'm afraid it's serious.'

Rachel stared at him in horror, her mind scarcely able to take in the terrible news.

'It's all right. I'm a policeman. Here's my identity card.' He held out a square of plastic with his photograph and an official stamp on it.

'What about my father?' Rachel asked as she got into the car.

'He'll be along soon. We've contacted him.' The man slammed the car door. 'I'm Inspector Smith, by the way.'

It wasn't until they reached the M1 that Rachel became suspicious. Inspector Smith had told her that her mother had fallen from a ladder whilst cleaning the windows.

'Which hospital did you say she was in?' Rachel asked.

'I don't believe I said, dear,' smiled Inspector Smith, slowing the car on to the hard shoulder of the motorway. 'Perhaps I'd better explain. By the way, there are child locks on both the back doors of the car, which make it impossible to open them from the inside.' He produced a long piece of thick string and turned round to kneel on his seat and face her. 'Rachel dear, if you scream or struggle, I'm afraid you will never see your mother and father again.' He grabbed her hands viciously and held them powerless in one hard bony one of his own, while with the other he began to wind the string round her wrists. Rachel gasped and began to struggle. Her watch came loose and fell to the floor of the car. Inspector Smith slapped her across the face. 'Keep still, Rachel dear, or it will be the worse for you. I am going to lock you up.' He laughed, showing pointed teeth. 'I'm going to lock you up where no-one can find you.' The string pulled tight. Rachel sobbed in panic. The traffic hummed past in an endless flow. Could no-one see her? Could no-one see what was happening?

'Why are you kidnapping me?' she demanded, trying to keep her voice firm. 'We're not rich. My parents can't give you a lot of money.'

Inspector Smith glanced back as he started the car, and smiled at her coldly.

'Your father is a bank manager, dear. He has access to millions of pounds. I'm sure he wouldn't mind quietly removing half a million and giving it to me, if he knows you will be killed otherwise.' With a chilling laugh Inspector Smith smoothly steered the car into the stream of traffic and began the long drive north.

Chapter 16

Rachel regained consciousness to find Leon and the old tramp dragging her between them across the sand. The tramp's thickly mud-coated hands held her tightly by the upper arm, and Leon supported her by the shoulders.

'I don't blame the lass for keeping away from the bluebottles,' puffed the tramp. 'Nothing but trouble, they ain't. Not catch me within a mile of 'em. They still reckon I swindled the dole money twenty years ago. Never forget, they don't. They'll have her locked up in no time. Quick as a flash. Bob's yer uncle. Never seen again.'

'Hang on a minute,' Leon interrupted. 'I think she's woken up.'

'Thank heavens. This is just about finishing me off.'

Rachel struggled to free herself. 'I can manage,' she croaked feebly, standing up.

'Phew.' The tramp blew out his cheeks and his alcohol-laden breath nearly knocked her down again.

'Come on,' urged Leon. 'Let's get up into the cave if you're both so worried about the police. They'll not find you there because they've looked there once already. What were you doing up the cliff, Rachel?'

'I wanted to visit the tower. I thought it might help me to remember.' Rachel abandoned all pretence as she struggled to climb the rocks to the cave. The tramp seemed to be having even more difficulty and Leon had to help them both.

'Remember? You said that once before. What do you mean?'

They all collapsed breathless on to the sandy floor of the cave.

'I've lost my memory, Leon. At least I had . . .' A violent fit of shivering overcame her. 'I thought . . . I thought the police were after me, but now I'm not so sure.'

The old tramp slid his eyes nervously to and fro as though expecting a policeman to leap out of the shadows. Leon stared at her, then took the newspaper out of his anorak pocket.

'Rachel, my reading ain't so good. I got this paper because my Dad wanted to see if his advert for the ponies was in. I think you'd better read it though, since it's something to do with you.'

Rachel took the proffered paper. 'Thanks.' She smoothed out the front page. The photograph of her was last year's school one. RACHEL CAVENDISH, STILL MISSING IN THE NORTH-WEST said the headline. "Although the car believed to have been involved in her kidnapping was found crashed on the A6 near Penderdale earlier this week, bank manager's daughter Rachel Cavendish has still not been found, and fears for her safety are growing. Numerous sightings have been reported since police released her name and photograph, after their initial news clampdown designed to thwart false information and the kidnappers' desire for publicity. It is believed that one kidnapper was treated at Lancaster Royal Infirmary, and released before his identity was realised. Police now fear that he may try to find Rachel before they do, in order to silence her and avoid identification. Anxious relatives from Walker's Tower Grange, Penderdale, and Rachel's own desperate parents who are staying there, are joining in the search."

Rachel looked up. Leon and the tramp were watching her.

'I think you were right, Leon. I haven't been quite all there. Perhaps I'd better explain, then we can go to the police station.'

The tramp backed away looking horrified, but sidled back as Rachel began her story.

'So you see,' she concluded eventually, 'I've been running away from this Inspector Smith thinking he was a policeman and I was the criminal, but he was only *pretending* to be a policeman . . .'

There was a sound outside.

'He must be chasing you to try and shut you up permanently.'

'Shhh. What was that?'

They all listened, and Leon edged them back into the far, dark section of the cave. The tramp's shuffling sounded very loud.

Rubber-soled shoes squeaked on the stones. Briefly a familiar shadowy silhouette showed in the entrance. It was Inspector Smith.

Chapter 17

'We're trapped.' Rachel's voice was barely audible. A huge shadow now completely darkened the entrance, then briefly the light illuminated an extended arm. 'Oh no! He's got a gun!'

Leon tugged her arm.

'Follow me,' he mouthed, beckoning the old tramp. The figure in the entrance stood still, his eyes not adjusted to the darkness as theirs were. Rachel stared incredulously at the back of the cave towards which Leon was shepherding them. There seemed to be nowhere they could go. The cave wall looked invulnerable apart from a deep narrow crevice which ran from the floor to the ceiling. Leon began squeezing sideways into it.

'I can't get into that!' exclaimed Rachel, horrified.

'It's bigger on the other side.' Leon's voice was muffled because he was unable to turn his head to reply. There was a scrabbling in the entrance.

'Ah, Rachel dear. I can hear you back there. It's no good hiding from Inspector Smith, you know. Come along now. You can't get out.'

Rachel began to squeeze into the crevice after Leon, while the old tramp hopped from one foot

the one-legged man who washes his foot in Coke.'

The other two stared at her in astonishment, but the tramp seemed to perk up a little after that, much to Rachel's relief, as she was feeling far from steady herself.

They trudged round the perimeter of the cave until they reached a narrow opening on the far side.

'It's darker through here.' Leon no longer bothered to whisper. 'I'll just get me torch out.' He rummaged in his anorak pocket and produced an old fashioned flashlight. 'We'll have to go in single file and hold on to each other. It's steep and narrow so I'll go slowly. You two call out if you can't keep up.'

It was wet too. When Leon had gone through the opening Rachel ushered the old tramp ahead of her. The rough-shaped gap was the size of a small doorway. She followed behind, holding on to his coat. The walls were close enough for her to touch on either side at once, and felt slimy. Leon's torch beam danced ahead of them. The rock was slippery underfoot and a dank smell of wet earth filled her nostrils. They stumbled on. Rachel was beginning to feel more and more ill every minute. At least she was no longer hungry, she reflected. The mere thought of food was enough to make her sick.

At last the steep passage widened into another larger cave, with light filtering through the roof. It glinted on a row of small pools which lay in hollows of the rock. With a groan the old tramp sank on to a boulder by the wall.

'I'm done for, lad,' he said in a slurred voice. 'I can't go no further.'

They paused.

'I have to sit down too, Leon.' Rachel flopped down next to the old man, feeling the dampness through her jumper. Leon looked at them worriedly, his hands on his hips.

'Tell you what, I'll go and get some food and a flask of tea. It'll take me about two hours there and back. You two have a rest, then we'll go on later. Here, have the newspaper and the torch. He'll not be able to find his way into the caves from the far end, that Inspector Smith, and I doubt he'd have come through the crevice. He'll not find you, unless he's got someone local helping him.' Leon took the newspaper from his pocket and dropped it by Rachel's side, then he handed her the torch and turned and disappeared into the darkness.

Chapter 18

Rachel hoped that Leon was right. Listening uneasily for footsteps she slid into an uncomfortable doze. Half asleep and half awake, she understood at last that she had been kidnapped to force her father to pay a ransom from his bank. Instead he must have gone to the police. She had no reason to fear the police, only the phoney "Inspector" Smith. She had forced the car accident to try and escape in an area she knew, close to Penderdale, where Aunt Pauline, Uncle Roger and Cousin Emily lived in Walker's Tower Grange, their rambling grey house a mile from the cliffs. She slid into sleep, and in her dream she walked in the garden with Emily. The twisted trees which sloped away from the bottom of the garden towards the woods and the cliff edge were like the tough, weatherbeaten Cumbrian forebears about whom Aunt Pauline talked so much. They had lived in their bleak, wild tower until it began to crumble around them, then they had built the new house further inland.

Holidays at Penderdale had always been wonderful. She and Emily were the same age and looked alike. They explored the woods and caves together, roaming across the pitted limestone crags, but saving their best games for the ruined tower on the clifftop. On summer evenings they and their parents had barbecues on the paved area by the old stone well. In the hall hung great great grandfather Walker's portrait, his black-bearded figure against the tower as it had once been. Rachel's dream blended back into reality, a raging thirst forcing her awake. She was sweating and feverish, and her bones ached. Awkwardly she eased herself into a more comfortable position.

The tramp was dozing too. She shone the torch on to him anxiously. His breathing was rasping and difficult and, despite the dirt and the semi-darkness, he looked very pale. With every breath his lips fluttered outwards, then sagged in again. She hoped Leon would not be long.

She decided to read the newspaper, but the words wavered in front of her feverish eyes. Perhaps she would feel better if she had a drink. Water was dripping somewhere within earshot, and it sounded temptingly fresh and cool, in contrast to the slimy uninviting water in the rock pools. Three more tunnels led out of the cave, in addition to the one from which they had emerged and the one into which Leon had disappeared. She shone the torch into each of them. The persistent tap-tap-tapping of the water seemed to come equally loudly from all of them, but one was too narrow and another too low and waterlogged, so she chose the middle of the three. The torch's small circle of light seemed dimmer now. She hoped the battery was not going to run out on her. In the blackness of the tunnel she had to feel with her hands in places, but the dripping drew her on. Her mind began to feel hazy and confused. Everything seemed unreal. Might this all be only a dream?

She passed through a cavern where a strange phosphorescence gleamed from the walls with green light. In another, dim daylight seeped from high up.

Abruptly there was more light ahead, and a dead end. Feeble sunshine came diagonally from far above. Rachel moved forward cautiously. She had arrived now. She had reached the dripping. It echoed loudly, round and round the confined space. She stopped in astonishment. Ahead of her was a brick wall.

In two places the bricks had crumbled and fallen out. One place was high above her head where the light came in, and the other was at the level of her shoulders. In bewilderment she stuck her head through the hole and looked up. A drop of water splashed into her eye. Suddenly she understood. This was a well shaft. The bricks continued round in a circular formation, and far above she could see the wooden well head with its suspended bucket. The circle of light seemed very far off. It made Rachel realise how far underground she was.

Holding out her hands she caught a few drips of water which were coming from a pipe above her head. It tasted sweet and clear and very good. The circle of light wavered above her as she became dizzy with craning her neck. She frowned. Surely there was something overlapping the edge of the tiny disc of sky up there. The something moved. Rachel leaned further out. Ferns grew from crevices in the brickwork, and the well was clearly old and unused. Rachel began to ease herself back into the tunnel when suddenly a deep hissing voice spoke all around her.

'Won't you have a cup of tea?' it said.

Rachel gasped and jumped back into the tunnel, banging her head. Who had said that? Was the tunnel haunted, or was she really going mad at last, because truly there was nothing she would have liked more than a cup of tea.

'Hello?' she croaked, her voice seizing up in her hot, parched throat.

'Goodbye then,' boomed the voice. Oh no, it was mocking her. It must be able to see her. Rachel turned to run, but where? Four different tunnels confronted her.

'Ho ho ho!' chortled the voice. Rachel backed against the brick well shaft and echoes of the laughter seemed to vibrate through her. Suddenly she closed her eyes and began to laugh too. Of course, it was the well shaft. They always created echoes. She remembered how she and Emily used to shout down the one at Walker's Tower Grange to hear their own distorted voices coming back up at them. Even if one were only sitting on the top or walking to and fro nearby, the well could sometimes seize one's voice and boom it back at one. There must be people up there. She looked up again. The shape overlapping the edge was shifting to one side. Another was joining it. People were up there, sitting on the edge of the well. Would they help her? Was there any way they could get her up? Suddenly voices boomed around her again.

'It's very kind of you to come and help with the search, Mrs Pilsbury. I hope Mr Fish can manage without you for the day.'

'Oh, it's my pleasure, Mr Cavendish, I'm sure. It's the least I could do. I felt involved, what with the poor little mite coming to the shop like that. If only I'd known. I expect she's completely deranged, what with all she's been through. Oh hello, dear. How are you feeling? What a strain all this must be.'

The bottoms had moved round again, and a woman's voice spoke.

'Hello, Mrs Pilsbury. Thank you. Oh, I'm not feeling too bad.'

'Mum!' Rachel tried to scream, craning upwards. 'Mum! Mum!' But her voice had gone. Her throat was swollen and silent. In desperation she hammered on the side of the well. This was the well at Walker's Tower Grange, and safety lay just above her. No-one heard her.

Chapter 19

It was quite easy finding her way back to the cavern with the rock pools where she had left the old tramp. Rachel realised that with a bit of practice one could probably get to know one's way around the cave system quite well. Perhaps when all this was over Leon would bring her down again, and Emily too. The drink of spring water, and the sound of her parents' voices, had lightened Rachel's spirits a lot. She shone the torch round the rock pool cave, then frowned and shone it again. The old tramp was not there. Slowly, fear like ice crept into Rachel's bones.

'Tramp? Tramp?' she whispered hoarsely, realising that she did not know his name. Her voice bounced off the brown-veined ceiling, but there was no reply.

Had Leon returned while she was gone, and taken the tramp to safety? Had he been unable to find her? Was she left down here alone? Or worse still, was it Inspector Smith who had spirited the tramp away? Rachel edged back against the clammy wall and shone her torch hopefully into all the dark crevices. The newspaper still lay by the boulder where she had dropped it. She picked it up. Her own face looked back at her, the year before last's school photograph this time, with her side teeth missing. KIDNAP VICTIM RACHEL CAVENDISH said the caption. Rachel looked towards the far tunnel, down which Leon had gone when he left them an hour ago.

'Leon?' she whispered. Behind her the water still dripped. No other sound disturbed the ancient, dark honeycomb of rock. Her torch seemed dimmer suddenly. The battery was definitely failing.

Well, she would just have to find her own way out, she decided. Listening once more for any clue as to the tramp's whereabouts, a shuffle, a grunt, a wheeze, she set off.

This tunnel was steep, and soon became loose and pebbly underfoot, making Rachel slip and stumble. After a few metres it opened up and became a narrow platform round the side of another cave. At the far side a sheer cliff of slimy rock stretched above her head to the next opening. Slithering and grazing her knees Rachel scrambled up it. Suddenly, at the top, her foot lost its toehold in a crevice and she fell sideways, knocking the torch against a rocky outcrop. Its glass splintered and its dim beam became a vague mosaic pattern with hardly any light at all. Laboriously Rachel struggled her way to the top of the rockface again, and levered herself into the low opening. Light. There was light ahead. She began to crawl, ignoring the gravel which embedded itself in her knees. Clump, clump, hand, knee, hand, knee. A spider. A dear fat beautiful brown spider was sitting in a crack of the rock. The passage became lower and bent to the left. Rachel lay down flat on her stomach and wriggled along. Her head was in the bracken before she knew it.

For a moment Rachel just lay and looked at the leafy barrier ahead of her. Green light shone through it and another spider fled along a frond, alarmed by her sudden appearance. Rachel picked it up and put it gently on the rock at her side. Then she blundered forward into the light.

She was out. The late afternoon sunshine dazzled her eyes and the fresh wind blowing across the moors caught at her hair. She half-sat half-lay, breathing in the wild peaty smell of freedom.

The bracken had snapped back into place behind her and the rock from which she had emerged now looked innocently solid again. Rachel breathed a shuddering sigh of relief and raised her eyes to look around the boulder. On the far side of it stood Inspector Smith.

Chapter 20

For a long moment they stared at each other, then Rachel turned to run. At once rough arms seized her from behind, and a calloused hand clamped viciously over her mouth. Rachel kicked backwards at her attacker's shins, but his grip only tightened, making her teeth dig agonisingly into her top lip. She opened her mouth and bit his hand hard. With a sharp curse, her assailant hurled her on to the springy bracken and she saw him for the first time. It was the scarred, dark-haired man who had driven the hedge cuttings truck.

Rachel began to get up, then she saw his gun. It was the first gun she had even seen properly in real life. It was small and black and shiny and utterly terrifying. The man was pointing it at her forehead. Coaxingly his bitten thumb eased the safety catch up with a click, and he smiled. Inspector Smith joined him, one eyebrow raised.

'Well Rachel, if you've quite finished. You've led us quite a chase, my dear. Never mind. Inspector Smith always wins in the end. Tie her up too, Frank. I'll get the car.'

Too? Frank dragged her behind the rock and

Rachel groaned as she saw Leon and the tramp lying there, bound hand and foot, and gagged. Roughly Frank tied her wrists and ankles with nylon string, then pulled a woollen scarf tightly across her mouth until she felt as though her head were being sawn in two. She lay limply, too weak now to resist. A car started nearby and came bouncing towards them across the bracken.

Rachel looked at Leon. His face was streaked with mud and tears, and his eyes were sullen and furious. He attempted to smile at her, then frowned and grunted in the direction of the tramp. The old man was breathing with difficulty, his eyes shut and a waxen pallor showing beneath the grime on his face. He was clearly very ill. Rachel nodded back at Leon despairingly.

'Get up!' snapped Inspector Smith, kicking Leon in the ribs as the car lurched unevenly towards them. His companion got out.

'I still reckon we should finish them off here,' Frank muttered. Inspector Smith scowled.

'Don't be a fool, Frank. We can't risk the bodies being found. The forensic blokes can practically tell your name and address just from a hair on someone's sweater. They've got to disappear without trace. Lake Coniston's nice and deep in the middle . . .'

Inspector Smith and Frank bundled Rachel, Leon and the tramp violently on to the back seat of the car. The door slammed and the engine roared. Rachel tried to move. Leon's knee was digging into her shoulder and her face was pressed against the tramp's evil-smelling raincoat. The nylon cord around her wrists and ankles was chafing painfully, and a numb throbbing was beginning in her toes and fingers.

The car began to move, jerking slowly forward then picking up speed as it reached the road. Leon was trying to bite through his gag, but only succeeded in working it further into his mouth. Bits of the wool from Rachel's gag were tickling her nose, and it began to run. She sneezed a sneeze which backfired into her throat almost choking her.

'Shut up!' Inspector Smith snarled.

It was like the previous journey. Rachel lay in the back in despair. By wriggling upwards she could see between the front seats and out of the front window, and she realised that they were on the road down from Rownside Heights towards Rownside itself.

'Turn left at the bottom, towards the M6, Frank,' Inspector Smith muttered. Suddenly he swore. 'Ye gods, a road block!'

At that moment the sirens began.

'Straight across! Take the Rownside road!'

Frank accelerated across the road junction. The hedges flashed past in a blur. Behind them the sirens of two police cars joined in a spine-chilling chorus, and the blue lights flashed through the interior of their car. The outskirts of Rownside flew towards them. Frank did not slow down. From her peephole between the seats Rachel could see the speedometer reaching ninety, ninety-five, a hundred miles an hour. Horrified pedestrians fled from their path. Cars swerved with screeching tyres as they hurtled across the red traffic lights. Suddenly another police car appeared ahead of them. Frank bumped the car up on to the pavement with a jolt which jumbled them all together, then jammed his foot down again and drove the wrong way round the market cross. The Penderdale signpost shot past, then they were on the Penderdale road. One of the police cars edged ahead. Frank rammed it with a sound of grinding metal. For a moment the back of their car swung wildly, then straightened, leaving behind the clank of a falling bumper.

It was the route the hedge cuttings truck had taken. The hill and the bend approached. Rachel moaned in terror as the back of the car veered uncontrollably again on the sharp corner, and they were thrown on top of each other in the back.

The sirens were close again as they entered Penderdale. The little promenade was quiet. It was teatime, but doors began to open as the howling procession went by. Next to the railings the shrimp stall stood unattended. Their car caught it a glancing blow on the corner, and sent the shrimps cascading into the air like a pink fountain. Sounding like hailstones, they came down on the windscreen of the car. Frank cursed and turned the windscreen wipers on. They jammed amid the pile of tiny fishes. The car swerved, and Rachel and Leon closed their eyes as the tyres screamed and the wheels hit the pavement. The sea and the drop to the sand hurtled towards them, then the green-painted railing slammed into the side of the car with a grating thud. For a moment the car teetered on the edge, then it was still. The railings held.

Inspector Smith and Frank had gone. They were out of the car and running before the police vehicles had even stopped. Shaken and shocked, Rachel and Leon huddled in the back seat while a policeman and a policewoman leaned in and untied their hands and feet, and removed their gags. A large crowd had begun to gather outside.

'He's ill,' Rachel croaked, pointing to the tramp and fighting off waves of dizziness. The policewoman felt her forehead.

'Hm. So are you, my dear. Bert, better call for an ambulance.'

Suddenly the sound of gunfire came from further along the promenade. The policewoman straightened up sharply.

'They've got em, ma'am,' called Bert from in front of the car. 'No-one injured.'

Leon helped Rachel out, and they watched as Frank and Inspector Smith were led past them in handcuffs and pushed unceremoniously into one of the police cars. Another siren sounded from the direction of the Rownside road, and an ambulance appeared with its lights flashing. Men with stretchers and red blankets climbed out, and the tramp was gently lifted on to one and carried away. A corner of his dirty macintosh hung out from under the red ambulance blanket. An oxygen mask was placed over his face. Rachel watched in relief.

'I hope he enjoys this stay in hospital as much as he did his last one,' she mouthed to Leon, her swollen throat completely silent now. Leon grinned and nodded, supporting her with his arm. Together they lurched unsteadily over the road and into the ambulance.